DISPOSOPHOBIA

A black comedy about identity theft, lovers, liars & old phone bills

By James Murphy

DISPOSOPHOBIA

By James Murphy

Born in 1957, James Murphy grew up in the suburbs of South London. He graduated in Philosophy from the University of East Anglia at Norwich. He then worked in several different fields (sometimes literally), including journalism and teaching. During the 1980s, he lived in Tuscany. He recently moved to Sussex, his house having burned down in Hampshire (as per Nietzsche's metaphorical Vesuvian exhortation). He is married with a son.

By the same author

Crash the Bus (novel)
To Hell in a Handcart (play-script)
Stroke (play script)
The Poets (play script)
The Misanthropist's Secret Love Life (poetry)
The art of Exile (poetry)
Wrongdoing (poetry)
Handbook for the Damned (cultural & literary criticism)

DISPOSOPHOBIA

James Murphy

Published by The Heretic's Press
London
www.hereticspress.co.uk

ISBN 978-1-9996149-0-4

© 2018 James Murphy
Published by The Heretic's Press
www.hereticspress.co.uk

Front & back cover photo courtesy of Heretics Press
Front and back cover design
*by Chris Derrick @*www.unauthorizedmedia.com

DISPOSOPHOBIA – Preface

"You must have chaos in you to create a dancing star," averred Nietzsche - not expressly referencing the hoarder's flat I visited in Woking a couple of years back. However, had that sublime analyst of the creative urge come cleaning with me that hot summer's day in the jaded suburbs of outer London I feel sure he would've understood the grotesque misappropriation of his brilliant aphorism for the purposes of explaining this play's existence.

Disposophobia is an attempt to wrest some sort of habitable, creative design from the chaos of odd-jobbing, a chaos both metaphorically and actually real in the context of the hoarder's flat I was contracted to help clean and clear that day. Make no mistake, a hoarder's house presents a very real emotional challenge: to step inside it is to confront some powerful forces of psychological dissolution. Indeed, a strange dynamic is at work in the hoarder's dysfunction, one which would, in the name of keeping everything, actually lose all sense of meaning. By analogy, then – and ironically - it seems that to retain some sense of value we all have to learn to reject things – to select not just from our possessions, but also from our memories and even our emotions; and insodoing discover that to let some things go is to keep the things that matter.

In this respect, perhaps we are all hoarders to a certain degree; all trying to hold onto people, places, times, experiences and associations, and insodoing we're all occasionally prone to self-delusion. Moreover, if, figuratively speaking, keeping secrets and hiding our true feelings from each other are psychological forms of hoarding, then Disposophobia is about three possessive individuals who collide in the blind spots of their relationships with each other. In the ensuing chaos, just who is hoarding what becomes disastrously clear for all of them.

James Murphy 2018. *Nb - place names have been changed.*

Cast list

Sophie - a painter and poet, currently scratching an existence as a part-time cleaner, late 20s.

Karl - Sophie's boyfriend and occasional co-worker, very early 30s. Been on the verge of breaking through in the music business for longer than either of them cares to remember.

Tony - an eccentric, comfortably-off, though somewhat penny-pinching hoarder, late 50s/early 60s.

Place – A London flat

Time – Contemporary

Act 1. *A hot summer's day. The shabby communal hall of a Victorian mansion block of flats in Putney, South-West London. In the semi-darkness we hear two cleaners, Karl and Sophie, groping about trying to unlock the door to a flat.*

Sophie   *(calls softly)* Tony!

Karl   You sure it's the right key?

Sophie   'Course it's the right bloody key! Probably forgotten we're coming.

Karl   *(shouts)* Tony!

Sophie gestures to him sharply.

Sophie   Don't shout. He hates strangers… - I bet he's asleep.

Karl   Or dead. - Try turning it the other way.

Sophie   You're standing on my foot!

Karl   - Clockwise, I said! Let me have a go! *(he takes the key and drops it)*

Sophie   Brilliant, now you've lost it! *(He hits the light-switch)*

Karl   Don't any of these lights work!?

Sophie   Nope! Now what, genius? *(He searches for the key on the floor)*

Karl   Got it! *(Pause)* There! *(He gets door open)* Jesus! What a stench!

Sophie   I told him to open the windows before we came *(shouts)*– Tony! Tony, we're here! Tony, I'm going to open the windows! Are you awake?

They enter the room. Lights up on Karl and Sophie standing upstage facing the audience, staring into a room which is knee-deep in newspaper, rubbish, boxes, plastic bags of all kind. Disconnected bits of broken hi-fi and computers also litter every corner. Karl and Sophie stand in shock surveying the job that faces them. At centre stage there

1

is a table with a shredder on it, and two chairs. At stage right, sits a broken sofa, its stuffing hanging out. Mid-stage left, a fridge and sink constitute a galley kitchen, the sink is piled high with dirty crockery, pots and pans. They put down their equipment. Karl kicks a channel through the mess. Sophie goes over to the fridge.

Karl   The flies in here!

Sophie   Open the windows! - *(reads note)* He's gone out.

Karl   - And I was so looking forward to meeting him.

Sophie   He'll be back. He likes to supervise us.

Karl   Supervise - the man who did this?!

Sophie   I've seen it worse: depends how long we leave it between visits.

Karl   When did you last come, the Vietnam war?

Sophie   Here, open a few of these black bags for me – newspapers first. *(she looks around)* It's a nice flat - potentially.

Karl   Absolutely. Shabby-chic - half a ton of shit fitted as standard… Seriously - doesn't he ever throw *anything* away?!

Sophie   Nope: hoards it all: that's why the agency sends us in.

Karl discovers the shredder

Karl   What's this? A hoarder with a shredder – Very postmodern.

Sophie   To prevent identity theft - so he says.

Karl   Who'd want to steal *his* identity!? *(looks inside)* Ah but of course: the shredder is empty. And why---?

Sophie   Probably broken ---

Karl   - Because he never had an identity to shred! Elementary my dear Watson!

Sophie looking around again.

Sophie   Actually it *is* a bad as ever. Christ knows what I'm going to tell the agents.

Karl   The truth?

Sophie   I'd hate to get him chucked out. The bedroom's even worse. He won't let us go in there. There are cobwebs the size of fishing nets - piles of old unwashed clothes. Now they did stink!

Karl   Which door?

Sophie   That one.

Karl tries the door. Sophie starts to sort through her equipment.

Karl   Locked. – Bloody Bluebeard.

Sophie   Minus the wives.

Karl   - Or maybe you just missed them in the debris; maybe they're hanging up behind his dry cleaning.

Sophie   Keep your voice down.

Karl   - Why? He's not here - or maybe he's buried alive: *(shouts)* Tony! Maybe he's in the bedroom diddling his plastic dolly to death – assuming he can find her.

Sophie   Karl! - He's still a client for god's sake!

Karl   Client or not, he's mad! Gotta be.

Sophie   Maybe. But he's not stupid. He's very well read, actually. Knows a ton of stuff about art.

Karl   Yeah, but is he safe, this art connoisseur of yours?

Sophie   'Course he is! Harmless. - Bit touchy maybe…

3

Karl   About what?

Sophie   Stuff. I don't know - things – family: the past. He tells crazy lies - don't pick him up on them! Told me his mother was a spy last time. Says the first thing that comes into his mind sometimes. Told me I looked fat once. Had to laugh.

Karl   - Well as long as he doesn't start *doing* the first thing that comes into his mind – *(comes across a claw-hammer which he picks up)* - like staving our heads in with a claw-hammer

Sophie   He's just got a screw loose.

Karl   Thank you Professor Freud. *(speaking in cod German accent he mimes hitting Sophie on the head with said hammer)* Und if his screw falls out, vee heff eine kleine problem, nein? Wir haben, in fact, ein Psycho!

Sophie   You're in my way. *(They do an accidental pas-de-deux trying to get round each other. He makes as if to waltz. She stops.)* Just put the mops over there. We'll start with the kitchen. No, actually *you* will. You'll have to wash up first. There's a mountain of it. He lets it all pile up.

Karl goes over to the galley kitchen area where the tottering architecture of crockery & pans greets him.

Karl   Oh Christ. It's no good. I'm going to be sick.

Sophie   Well do it in the sink please.

Karl   There's no room!

Sophie   Wait 'til you see the loo.

Karl   This is a health risk!

Sophie   What did you expect? He's a hoarder.

Karl   Dirty sod, you mean.

Sophie   Yes, but he's our dirty sod, so can we just get on with it?

Karl   Christ. – If I'd known it was this bad I'd've…

Sophie   You'd've what?

Karl   I'd've stopped you coming, that's what.

Sophie   And lose the contract with the agency.

Karl   Bugger the agency.

Sophie   And our flat too, I suppose.

Karl   We won't lose the flat.

Sophie   That's not what you said yesterday.

Sophie starts bagging up old newspapers.

Karl   I was depressed yesterday. Things'll work out. They always do.

Sophie   Because *I* work.

Karl   Oh don't start… the band is what it is – it's a long-term thing.

Sophie   So I noticed. Put these by the door, will you? They need recycling.

She passes him a small mountain of egg cartons.

Karl   Recycling, eh? Wonderful thing a social conscience…

He takes them out, and calls back to her.

Karl   Did I tell you we had an A and R man at the gig last night? Tommy recognised him: kept coming in and out apparently. Taking notes. He didn't stay. Prick.

Sophie   What's new.

Karl   Jesus, you're so bloody miserable today. Don't tell me: time-of the-month crap.

Sophie   No, Karl, it is not 'time-of-the-month crap.'

5

Karl   What then? If you've got something to say, say it. We agreed: tell the truth - all the time.

Sophie remains silent.

So?

Sophie   So what? Look I'm fine. I'm just … Can we just get on with it? *(She attacks the litter grimly.)* - Christ knows it's a big enough drag without spinning it out!

Karl   This is terrible. I mean, you said it was bad - but this! Why didn't you tell me? *(she glares at him)* Well, you *did* tell me! I'm just saying: there's gotta be something better.

Sophie   Such as?

Karl   Anything! What about that bookshop?

Sophie   That's gone. I'd've heard.

Karl   A bar, then.

Sophie   I'm not waiting on tables again!

Karl   All right then – an office, for chrissake!

Sophie   I can't stand offices. How many times have I gotta tell you: clockwatching all day. Drives me insane: Look: *you* don't want a career: *I* don't want a career. You want to play music: I want to paint – and write bloody stupid poetry that'll never be read - and here we are! *(beat)* Anyway, the bad contracts pay more.

(pause)

Karl   We *will* get through this, Sophie.

Sophie   So you keep saying.

Karl   This band is different: people are coming. There's real interest - I promise you. *(she looks at him)* What's that look for?

Sophie   I thought we said no more promises.

Karl   So it's all my fault.

Sophie   I never said that ---

Enter Tony, bustling in with several bags. He doesn't see Karl at first.

Tony   Never said what? - No! I'm being previous! Introductions first! Sophie! Lovely to see you again! Sorry I'm late – and sorry about the mess, been meaning to clear it up all week. Just been so busy with other stuff. Have you had a coffee? I'll make you a tea. I've got some super organic flapjacks! - Oh hallo, you would be…?

They are both momentarily dumbfounded by the innocence of Tony's good mood.

Sophie   Karl: he's my partner, Tony. Helping instead of Suzie – she's ill.

Tony   Oh, sorry to hear that. I like Suzie. *(to Karl)* 'Partner' as in business?

Sophie   We live together. You remember I told you - we'd got back together.

Tony   Ah yes, of course! Lucky man! She's a wonderful lady, your Sophie! Shouldn't be wasting her time on this sort of thing. – Though I'm glad she does, of course, from an entirely selfish point of view.

Karl   Sophie does this part-time. Very part-time, actually. She paints.

Tony   Of course - and writes! We have right old discussions, don't we Soph'? Modern art versus classical. Abstract v representation-a-lism – I can never say that right! - I didn't mean to cause offence.

Sophie   None taken, is there Karl? *(beat)*

Tony   Yes, well, if there's anything I can do to help.

Karl   You could live normally, that'd be a start.

Tony   Pardon?

Sophie   Help me with these magazines Tony! - Start dumping those by the bins, Karl.

Exit Karl squeezing past Tony, carrying out a pile of magazines in desultory fashion.

Tony   I'm sorry if I upset Bill. – Now, before you say anything: I know it's a mess!

Sophie   Karl.

Tony   Pardon?

Sophie   His name is Karl.

Tony   Karl – Of course! Strange: I don't usually get names wrong: I love names, tracing the etymology, I mean:– Karl - that's German isn't it? As in Marx, I mean.

Sophie   Probably. Now look Tony, these magazines ---

Tony   - Related to the Old English 'Churl', I think you'll find: 'a peasant or man of low birth' – hence our word 'churlish'. You're married to a churl, Sophie.

Sophie   Not yet, Tony.

Tony   Whereas you, Sophie, are a goddess!

Sophie   That's what all the boys say.

Tony   A goddess of wisdom – Sophia!

Sophie   And what about you, Tony? You must be the god of old magazines! Look at them! Half of them are unwrapped!

She examines them one by one.

Tony   Yes, I know: we'll get through some of those today: some of those *can* go.

Sophie   Like these: Henley: Royal Regattas 1960 - 2000! - Or this: Goodwood Festival of Speed 1990 - 2010! How did I miss these last time? - Now this one, I like: "A history of literary quotations – from Homer to Homer Simpson.'

Tony   Ah yes! Been very useful that one! - "Beauty will save the world!"… Tolstoy. - I have something of a photographic memory.

Sophie   Millennium Monster truck? - Monster trucks?

Tony   They can surmount large obstacles. I admire that in a machine – and a man!

Sophie   American Shark Fisherman 1985 onwards! – Tony, you know what the agents said about printed matter: you can keep a fair collection of the photographic ones, which we know you like, but the others must go. All these newspapers! It's a fire risk. Not to mention the bills – and these boxes *(she rifles through a box of letters)* – letters to the electricity board from … 1971!

Tony   Ah now those I'm keeping! *(He gently takes them from her)* – Some personal ones mixed in with that lot. *(beat)* Look, Sophie, I know I've got… a problem… as some people see it. But you've got to keep old letters…. they're records. They remind you of who you used to be, who you used to love! - Bills, receipts - how else are you s'posed to know what you paid for, what you used to like? - No, I can't let go of them, it wouldn't be right. They're as much a part of me as – well, the person standing in front of you …I mean, who's to say I'm more real now than I used to be? We're *not* just the present, *are* we! - Or memory wouldn't matter. Sometimes the past seems *more* real than what happens in the present. Take that toy car. Now I know it's just a silly old thing, battered and bruised with its paint all off – but that's a Dinky 23e, a rare one - the land record car! I can tell you exactly where I was when I got that! What my mother was wearing. The smile on her face. That's why I keep things, if you must know. - If I forget them, how am I supposed to I know who I am?" *(Sophie begins to object.)* I know. I know. Well you'll help me get rid of a couple of things today. We'll go through them together. And I've got the shredder working again! For some of the other stuff, I mean.

9

Re-enter Karl

Tony cont.   Ah Bill! I'm really sorry if I offended you - I didn't mean to cast any aspersions.

Karl   It's 'Karl.'

Sophie   Forget it, Tony: We're a bit stressed today – late night, and all that.

Tony   Ah well that I can relate to! I suffered constant stress in my job on the Underground. Some of the public you have to deal with! City gents, ladies straight from Knightsbridge shops effing and blinding - you wouldn't believe it! Talk about industrial language! Enough to make a docker blush. That's why I don't use it myself. At least never in public. I'm no saint I admit, but there my conscience is clear!

Karl   Unlike your room.

Tony   Ha – a joker!

Karl   Who? Me or You?

Tony   Ha - definitely a joker. I shall have to watch you.

Karl   Ah but then I might hide, Tony, say, in the New Forest over in that corner.

Karl bags up more paper.

Tony   Careful with that! That's my stationary corner: I know where everything is in this place. Let me see what you're throwing away. I need to see!

Sophie   Just show Tony what you're throwing away Karl.

Tony   Yes, then I can start shredding - I want to be of some assistance if I can. I don't expect you to do it all on your own. *(Snatches a paper out of Tony's hands and stores it)* - So what is it you do normally, Karl?

Karl   I'm a musician, Tony - normally.

Tony   Oh yes? I play a bit of keyboard myself! Play in a band?

Karl   Yes, I play in a band.

Tony   Brilliant. What sort?

Karl   Rock.

Tony   Ah! Heavy? A Goth are you? Like a bit of death metal? No, more Coldplay, yes? I used to love Progressive stuff myself – Soft Machine, Van der Graf Generator. Tastes change of course. - I've kept all my programmes though.

Karl   I'll bet you have.

Tony   Cream! - Ginger Baker: now he was a proper drummer!

Karl   Bit before my time, Tony.

Tony   No! Are you sure?

Karl   Give or take half a century.

Tony   Joker! - So, come on: what do you play?

Karl   Guitar.

Tony   Of course: the hair and the leather jacket! Still in fashion after all these years! Amazing. How old are you actually – if you don't mind me asking?

Sophie   *(looking ironically at Karl)* Stickler for the facts our Tony!

Karl   Thirty-one, as it happens.

Tony   Oh yeah I get it: thirty-one going on forty! Nothing like the big 'four-O' to sober you up, eh? Christ I remember when I turned forty ---

Karl   I'm not forty.

Tony   - I looked in the mirror. - Stood for about a minute in total silence, and I saw this face staring back. And when I smiled, it didn't smile back. And I thought 'Christ, I'm middle-aged!' Standing there with a pot belly, bald head – crows feet round the eyes!

Karl   I'm not forty.

Tony   Over half my life gone forever! God knows what on the horizon! Old Age disease and death, eh! It's not fair, is it? – the gap between a youthful mind and an aging body, I mean! – 'Mind the gap', eh? Actually that was me on that recording you used to hear on the Underground.

Sophie   Really?

Tony   They got me to use my posh announcer's voice: 'move down inside the carriage please, ladies and gentlemen. Mind the Gap!' – 'Course, that was some years back, before I moved into property development. – Don't get old, eh? I mean I feel twenty-one, but look at me! That's why I don't keep any mirrors in this place. Well, I've got one in the bathroom – but that's just for my teeth!

Sophie   I'm going in there in a minute Tony: so make sure you've got everything out that you need.

Tony   I shall indeed my dear! – Maybe I should get a facelift! What do you think Karl?

Karl   Cosmetic surgery's for losers, Tony.

Tony   Ah yes, losers. *(repeats distractedly)* Losers. Losers. Losers. – Well! We've all got something of that in us, I suppose, Karl, haven't we?

Karl   Have we?

Tony   Well you're not exactly famous yet, are you?

Karl   We've just been offered a deal, since you mention it.

Tony   Oh yeah? Great. Never too late, I suppose. You must be pleased, Sophie!

Sophie   He's going to take me away from all this, aren't you Karl?

Karl   So how old are *you*, Tony? *(Pointedly ironic)* If you don't mind me asking?

Tony   Sixty-four – and I look every bloody inch of it, I know. I've been trying to lose weight actually. But then at the end of the day you've got to be happy in your own skin: haven't you? Even if there is too much of it. – No, accept yourself, I say: accept who you are - and look your age. *(looks at Karl)* Well, dress your age anyway. Eh Karl? -Anyway, I'll go and clear the bathroom.

Tony exits to the bathroom

Karl   Did you hear that? 'Not exactly famous?' 'Dress my age!' Fucking cheek!

Sophie   *(smiling)* Well, you've got to admit - he's got a point.

Karl   What?

Sophie   That jacket.

Karl   What about it?

Sophie   Well it is a tad, how shall we say? - Duran Duran..?

Karl   Oh so you agree with our fashion guru, do you? Putney's own Christian Dior here!

Sophie   *(smiling)* He's got to you, hasn't he? I told you he was frank.

Karl   Frank, my arse! This shit is a total façade! God knows who this bloke is, but I'm telling you he's not the sweet little innocent you make out! – 'Frank'! Two can play at that game…

Sophie   *(Warningly)* Karl..!

Re-enter Tony

Tony   Yes, life's all about coming to terms with reality.

13

Karl   That's a big word, Tony.

Tony   Sorry?

Karl   Reality.

Tony   It is indeed! - And one which means different things to different people.

Karl   So what does it mean to you?

Sophie   Karl we really need to get on now.

Karl   How would it relate to, say, where you lived, for example?

Sophie   Tony, you can help by keeping out of the way.

Karl   - Given that we're all different behind closed doors. Public and private personas, I mean. There you are: one person out in the street, buying your neat bags of shopping, and then you get home and dump them all.

Tony   I don't dump anything. I do have standards, you know.

Karl   Really? I can't see any.

Tony   Ah but that doesn't mean there aren't any! It may look like a mess but I know where everything is in every inch of this place.

Karl   So what's over …. there – for example?

Tony   Where?

Karl   Behind that shredder.

Tony   That's an easy one: that's my cassette corner.

Karl   Right, right… - and over there?

Tony   That's where I keep my negatives.

14

Karl   Negatives, eh? Bit old paradigm, Tony.

Tony   Yes, well. - And my lenses. For my old SLR cameras, which, of course, I don't use so much anymore.

Karl   Of course not. - Mind if I have a look? *(Goes to corner)* Nope. Can't see them.

Tony   They're over there somewhere. *(Karl displaces a pile of letters, then picks up a glass 'snow-globe')* Careful with that! I've had that snow-globe since I was ten! And watch those letters, they're all in order! *(Karl drops a few)* Please. Can you stop that!

Sophie   He's only teasing, Tony.

Tony   Yes, well! It took me a long time to sort them out. They're all in order.

Karl   All right: keep your hair on. Didn't realise a sense of order was so important to you, Tony. You should watch that: can get to be a neurosis: being too tidy: obsessive-compulsive and all that. Maybe you should just let it all hang out a bit more.

Tony   *(poker-faced)* Ha ha. *(pause)* - Look, I've got problems with this flat! I just don't have enough room for the things I want to keep. – If I'm honest, it's the same with my house.

Karl   What house?

Sophie   You haven't got a house, have you Tony?

Tony   Well, I don't use it at the moment: not since my mother died. Unhappy memories – *(mimicking Karl)* "and all that."

Sophie   I'm very sorry to hear that, Tony – I mean, about your mum.

Tony   Yes, well, I haven't had the heart to go back. It's still got a lot of her stuff in it actually. Partly why there's not enough space there either!

Karl   Yes, but only 'partly', eh!

Tony   What?

Sophie   *(Quickly interjecting)* Well maybe we could help you with that too Tony!

Tony   Absolutely! I plan to sub-let it eventually, when I've had it cleaned. - I moved out when I realised it was just too small for my needs!

Karl   - Or maybe it's not the size of the place that's the problem Tony: maybe it's the size of your appetite for things! Maybe you'd have too many things for any place you lived in! I've got it! *(articulates deliberately)* - You need to throw some things away..!

Sophie   And that's what we're going to help you do today, Tony – aren't we Karl? *(she pushes past Karl with a glare on her way out with a black bag)*.

Tony   Well, that's right. I do need help. I want to be more tidy. - I want to keep this place more… - well, I just want to keep this place…. – I'll get some new tea. I'm sorry if the last lot was too weak. I'll put in a couple of extra bags.

He exits.

Karl   So! Tony's got another house full of shit to go with his flat full of shit! That really is obscene!

Sophie   What the fuck are you doing?

Karl   I'm being frank, Sophie. - You said he was frank. So I'm frank. What's the problem?

Sophie   The problem is you're upsetting him, which is making my job a fuck-sight more difficult.

Karl   Oh come on: bit of banter! Anyway, whose side are you on? - Why should you even have to do this job? Why is it acceptable that he leaves the place in a shit state for *anyone*? What's his landlady doing? Doesn't she care that he's completely ruined the place?

Sophie   The agency pays us to put it right. Anyway, he pays the rent.

Karl   Big deal.

Sophie   Yeah it is actually. Do you know how hard it is to get decent tenants?

Karl   'Decent?!'

Sophie   He pays the rent in full, every month, on time: and he pays me in cash: that makes him a decent tenant.

Karl   Not in my book.

Sophie   Yeah well who reads your book?

Karl   He needs help – serious help.

Sophie   From you.

Karl   No-one else is paying him any attention! You come and clean this shit up for him, but that's as good as saying it's OK for him to rubbish in the first place. – What if someone actually called him out on the way he lives? Maybe this mess is a cry for help?

Sophie   No Karl, it's a cry for a cleaner. You playing God with your amateur psychology is the last thing he needs.

Karl   All right: a good bollocking then! Someone to connect with him enough to tell him the truth: that's it's not OK to live like this! Forget detergent: – honesty, that's what this room needs, an industrial dose of it!

Sophie   Oh sure, I can hear Tony now: 'How honest Karl is! How wise! I must change my life immediately". - Case closed, Doctor Freud.

Karl   So what's *your* solution?

Sophie   *(holds up squeezy bottle)* This, Karl! I'm his cleaner not his confessor. I get ten quid an hour and then I go home and forget I was ever here.

Karl   Yeah, well maybe we should give him a bit of exposure therapy into the bargain!

17

Sophie   What?

Karl   Expose him to his fears…*(She looks at him)* - get him to face them - confront him with the facts!

Sophie   As you see them!

Karl   Well certainly not as he bloody well sees them! Look, he might change if he hears what people really think instead of just lying to him politely in the good old British way!

Sophie   You think so.

Karl   Why not? It works with a lot of them: Look it up in Wikipedia!

Sophie   *(mocking)* Wikipedia.

Karl   - Disposophobia, it's called.

Sophie   Disposophobia.

Karl   Otherwise known as Diogenes Syndrome.

Sophie   Diog---

Karl   The guy who lived in a barrel – you don't have to repeat everything I say.

Sophie   I just can't believe you're being so…

Karl   What?

Sophie   So…

Karl   Spit it out.

Sophie   Glib.

Karl   Glib?

Sophie   Mind-blowingly so.

Karl   I'm being glib?

Sophie   As glib as it gets.

Karl   OK, if I'm being glib, what are *you* being?

Sophie   A cleaner, Karl: - what I'm paid to be!

Karl   Just saying - gotta be worth a try.

Sophie   No. It hasn't! Jesus, that's it, isn't it: you really think you're going to revolutionise his life just because you've read Wikipedia!?

Enter Tony again carrying tea, sandwiches which Karl rejects.

Tony   Hallo again. Hope I'm not interrupting anything interesting?

Karl   This is Putney, Tony: it's not possible to interrupt anything interesting.

Tony   Not true actually, Marc Bolan was killed down the road in 1970: a sad moment indeed for modern music, as any real music lover would agree! And the Boat Race starts here every year! —And we had a murder down by the bridge only a week ago. A tramp: junkies, they reckon; what they expected to find on the poor old sod, god only knows. - All this knife crime! You fear for your life every time you go out these days. Young men in gangs. Nothing better to do than sell drugs and stab each other.

Karl   I think you'll find it's a bit more complex than that, Tony.

Tony   Never know *who* might be following you home!

Karl   Well, they'd 'luck out' if they broke in here, Tony! Must have a fortune stashed away. Where is it? Stuffed in this old sofa, I bet!

Tony   I don't keep cash.

Karl   'Bout the only thing you don't keep!

Tony   I'm not a miser.

Karl   Shame: we could have murdered you ourselves and dumped your body in 'stationary corner' without anyone ever finding you.

Tony   That's not funny.

Karl   No – but then nor is stationary corner.

Tony   Stationary Corner isn't meant to be funny: it's the closest I get to an office.

Karl   - The closest you get to anything in here! You should try using some of that paper, Tony: you know, write on it, then send it to someone: it's a very good, if old –fashioned invention. Called 'letter-writing'.

Tony   I do use it – all the time. I have a lot of correspondence to do now as it happens. I hope you don't mind if I sit here and write: can you clean around me? I'll tell you what! A bit of music! What do you say Soph? *(He goes over to CD player)*

Karl   - 'ee'.

Tony   Pardon?

Karl   Soph – ee. She doesn't like it being shortened.

Tony   *(To Sophie)* Don't you? You never told me that.

Karl   Yes, well there's a lot of things she never told you.

Tony   Really, Soph? Sophie, I mean. You don't like it?

Sophie   I don't mind.

Tony   There you see: you don't know everything about her! So! *(He puts on CD)* - I know: - a bit of Beach boys!

Karl   Oh yeah that'll cheer us up.

Tony   Good Vibrations!

The strains of said song duly rend the sultry atmosphere. Tony shouts over it.

20

Tony cont. I've always loved this one! Actually that is a very complex 'lead-in'. There! Listen to that chord progression: that's more subtle than anything the Beatles ever did.

The music plays until at least the end of the first chorus. Tony 'conducts' while Karl tries to wash up and Sophie continues tidying.

Sophie Can you turn it down a bit?

Tony Not to mention the sound Denis Wilson gets on the Moog! That was extremely innovative for the time!

Sophie What?

Tony I said it was ahead of its time! No-one was using Moogs in that way at the time!

Karl goes over to the CD player.

What are you doing?

Karl We can't hear ourselves speak!

He turns it off and as he does so knocks over a pile of CDs. Tony lets out a cry of muted anguish.

Tony Leave them alone!

Sophie Karl!

Karl All right: I'm doing it!

Karl starts to pick them up. Tony moves Karl brusquely aside and does the job himself. Sophie glares at Karl who goes resentfully back to the washing up. There is a heavy silence.

Tony I'm sorry I lost my temper. – I can't bear people moving things without asking me… *(Heavy pause)* - Shall I change the music? Something quieter! Joni Mitchell!

Karl   Oh for Chrissake! *(he hurls the filthy dishcloth aside, plates clatter. Silence as he paces.)*

- Do you *ever do any* washing-up?

Sophie   Karl! ….*(exaggerated calm)* Let's just get the job done, shall we?

Pause.

Karl   Why is it so hot in here? Like a goddam greenhouse.

Tony   South-facing. We get sun all day long. Lovely view of the trees! Actually I do find it too bright in here. That's why I keep the shades drawn.

Karl   I bet it is. *(He sits down, takes a deep breath)* -I need a drink.

Tony   I'll get you a some fruit juice: I've got Mango! *(Exit)*

Sophie   Yeah, you have a good rest Karl.

Karl sets out his cigarette stuff. Sophie glares at him.

Karl   *(pointedly)* Anyone mind if I have a roll-up?

Sophie   Go for it. No fire risk here.

Karl begins making his roll-up.

Don't push it, Karl.

Karl   Don't push what?

Sophie   You're being incredibly childish. Can't you be a bit more compassionate, for chrissake!

Karl   Compassionate!?

Sophie   If you really understood his problem you'd show a bit more kindness.

Karl I *am* being kind. A bit of 'tough love', that's what this bloke needs.

Tony returns with juice.

Tony I suppose I've got used to the heat.

Karl And the flies.

Tony I was born in India, actually.

Karl Oh well that helps.

Tony And then I can do one thing my mother couldn't do!

Karl What, only one?

Sophie Ignore him Tony. *(trying to calm the general tone)* What was it?

Tony What was what?

Sophie The one thing you could do your mother couldn't do?

Tony Oh – sweat! You know the saying: 'Men sweat, horses perspire but ladies glow…' - Actually, my mother really *couldn't* sweat. Her glands didn't work properly. So the poor dear got really hot. She had to sleep a lot in summer. Not so bad in winter. Poor old mum.

Karl Maybe there were other things she wasn't so good at either.

Sophie Karl…

Tony I don't think so.

Karl Well, she was a human being with human failings, Tony; no doubt she wasn't perfect.

Tony She was a bloody good mother!

Karl Yeah, but what if you're forgetting something?

Tony I remember everything about her.

23

Karl   But do you? Childhood's a distant memory for everyone, Tony. How do you know you're not forgetting something about the way your mother brought you up? How do I know *I'm* not? I'll tell you, it was only when my mother died that I discovered I had a lot of negative feelings for her. - What if *your* mother was actually a bit different from how you remember her? Memory plays tricks, after all.

Tony   What are you talking about? *(Glances at Sophie)* Listen to him!

Sophie   He's teasing you Tony! Karl, give it a break… I mean it.

Karl   We remember things the way we want, the way we need to. Some say the blacker things were in reality, the rosier we paint them.

Tony   I'm not painting anything rosy!

Karl   - And we all need to think well of our mothers.

Tony   I *do* think well of my mother.

Karl   Maybe you do. Maybe you can't afford not to? What if – and this is only a 'what if' - what if the way you keep this room is related to the way your mother brought you up. I mean rooms are very basic emotional things, maps of the heart, you might say, maps of who and where we are, with our possessions as reference points.

Tony   *(shaking his head in mock incomprehensibility)* I'm sorry….

Karl   Well it's not normal is it? I mean, I doubt there's another room in the whole of Putney like it. So there must be some reason why it's like this - why you choose to have it like this.

Tony   I like it like this.

Karl   Yes, but why? Why do you, Tony, I'm sorry I don't know your surname ---

Tony   Morris.

Karl   Why do you, Tony Morris, like a room the way nobody else in Putney likes it? The way nobody else in Putney would ever dream of having it! There's got to be a reason? I'm just saying it could - only could, mind! - have something to do with something in your childhood.

Sophie   Karl, for god's sake ---

Karl   - And more particularly the attitudes that were bred in you by the most important people in that childhood. I've got this theory! --- *(he gets up enthusiastically)*.

Sophie   Take it with a pinch of salt, Tony.

Tony   Salt's bad for your blood pressure.

Karl   - I reckon our parents ---

Tony   - And so is he!

Karl   - Our parents are the seminal event in our lives. And given that most of them are a disaster – how we deal with that disaster constructs our personalities.

Tony   I don't think I like your theories.

Sophie   You're not alone.

Karl   Look at the facts. Your mother is all-powerful. You come out of her body! She's the first human being you set eyes on! - Apart from the obstetrician and he's wearing a mask so he doesn't count. No, your mother takes you in her arms, and with one look says - 'you are the most important thing in the world!' - And suddenly the whole world comes into focus.

Tony   Babies can't see when they're born: everyone knows that.

Karl   *(Ignoring him)* She makes you the centre of the universe – Touch, smell, taste - she even feeds you from her body! Without her nothing exists. Your mother gives you your whole sense of self, your whole ego.

Tony   She certainly gave you one!

Karl   (*Ignoring him*) Take breastfeeding! - A baby learns its most basic sense of security on the breast; learns that love exists, that the universe is kind.

Tony   What is this: post-natal classes?

Karl   - On the other hand! - neurosis also begins at the breast – or lack of it.

Sophie   Karl is a shameless fan of Doctor Spock, Tony.

Tony   What's Star Trek got to do with it?

Karl   A lot actually, in a manner of speaking. Think about it: we exit the womb screaming: in total shock – like someone drowning in a stormy sea!

Tony   Very poetical.

Karl   We don't know what's happening, what's in store for us. It's chaos, right? The void! But a mother's love is a searchlight streaming down on us in that darkness. A rescue. Suddenly out of nowhere this feeling of warmth overcomes us - this sensation: like a warm wave that envelopes us: your mother's breast: soft, lovely to touch, feeding you with the sweet, warm milk of life…

Tony   I wasn't breast-fed actually.

Karl   (*turning to Tony*) There you go! - If we don't get rescued! If we're left in the dark, with the storm and sea raging, and the cold wind blowing…

Sophie   Yeah we get the picture!

Tony   My mother *couldn't* breastfeed: she had bad mastitis, it wasn't her fault.

Karl   I'm not saying it was!

Sophie   Lots of women don't breastfeed actually, for a variety of reasons.

Karl For chrissake I'm just using it as an example! - If they *don't* love us, if mothers and fathers abandon us - and most do –

Sophie Really? I don't think so.

Karl I'm talking about emotional neglect!- emotional abandonment in early childhood! - then it somehow proves to us, in the privacy of our own consciences, that we're worthless, that we deserve it, deserve to be abandoned. No-one can live with that thought. No-one... *(beat)* - So we lie….We paint our memories, colour them – redesign reality, renovate the decrepit relationships we had with our parents. I mean, look how hard it is to criticise your own parents to other people. It's taboo: the hardest thing in the world to turn round and say 'my mother was a complete cunt'.

Sophie Karl, I don't think ---

Karl It's true, Sophie: take your dad: total arsehole: a useless, self-obsessed megalomaniac drunk who left you all when you were eight. And yet you always find some way of excusing him.

Sophie I do not.

Karl You say, 'yes, but we had lovely holidays with him', or ' he flew kites with my brother.' All of which may be true, but it doesn't change the fact that he was a bastard, yet you can't say it without qualifying it in some way. Don't get me wrong, I do the same with my mother. Jesus, I'm sure Goebbels' kids loved him too, right at the moment he poisoned them in the bunker... - That book I read! By the daughter of the Auschwitz commandant! She admits he was evil, but she still says, 'but he was a good man in some ways', 'a kind father', 'during his tenure he improved conditions for the inmates', bla, bla, bla.' – that's what I'm saying: something in us can't bear to admit our parents might just be absolute, unadulterated monsters... – because it makes us stand alone.

Silence. They both look at him.

Well?

Sophie Well what?

27

Karl It's true. You can't deny it!

Tony Deny what?

Sophie What's it got to do with Tony?

Karl I'm saying if we're abandoned, then we'll surround ourselves with things to make us feel safe! A ton of rubbish! To shore up our identities. Prove we exist. Why do you think people go shopping? To renew their identities! Why do we surround ourselves with things we like? To confirm who we are!

Tony I know what you're trying to do. But it's stupid. - I'm going to the toilet.

He gets up and goes over to the toilet, calling back as he goes.

I'm not neurotic. *(Slams door and calls out)* And I don't have a mother complex!

Karl *(shouting back)* Fine! All settled then! Your life – this flat – all totally normal!

Sophie *(Calling out exaggeratedly for Tony to hear)* Karl hold this bag while I dump these newspapers!

As they crouch over the bag, the following dialogue is exchanged in a barely repressed, hissed whisper.

Sophie Karl if you don't stop this I'm out of here.

Karl What are you talking about?

Sophie Do you seriously think you're helping him!? - What's happening to you? Have you gone mad? This is someone you barely know! What gives you the right to come in here and throw your weight around?

Karl Because he's hiding something!

Sophie So what? It's his flat: he can hide whatever he wants!

Karl   Not if he submerges it in shit and then expects someone else to clean up!

Sophie   So ranting on about his mother solves everything, does it! Jesus, you haven't got a clue what she was like! What do *you* know about his relationship with her!

Karl   I wasn't ranting.

Sophie   - Not to mention that crap about my father!

Karl   It wasn't crap.

Sophie   It *was* the moment you mentioned it in public, Karl! These things are private! Intimate! Between people who know each other, trust each other! - *thought* they trusted each other!

Karl   So you're not even remotely curious why he's like this? It doesn't interest you in the slightest?

Sophie   Not while I'm cleaning his flat, no.

Karl   Look I'm not saying he's a pervert: I'm sure he's not! But you can't say he's normal.

Sophie   I've never said he was normal! But it's not up to you to diagnose him. – Why *are* you so bloody interested in him? Ask yourself that! Anyway, what do you know about Disposophobia? It might be nothing - a minor attitude problem. A nervous tick!

Karl   Come on: you heard him when I mentioned his mother.

Sophie   I heard you be bloody rude!

Karl   It's all down there! I promise you.

Sophie   What, Karl? Where? Where is this 'thing' he's hiding?

Karl   Buried a mile deep, that's where! Layers of memories! Weird emotions fossilised in the sediment! I'll bet it's Jurassic down there! I'll bet you this bloke's soul is a World Heritage Sight of special significance!

Sophie   And you're the man to excavate him!

Karl   Yup: the archaeology of the hoarder's mind! Stand aside.

He hurls another black bag full of rubbish across the room,

Sophie   And when you've dug him up, how are you going to stick Humpty Dumpty back together again? Have you thought of that? For Christ sake just leave him alone!

Enter Tony.

Tony   Do I hear the sounds of marital discord?

Sophie   We're not married.

Karl   Not yet.

Tony   I forgot: I was supposed to pick up my old laptop from the menders today. I'll only be gone a few minutes.

Karl inspects one of Tony's computers.

Karl   You're well kitted out with replacements, Tony, I'll give you that.

Tony   Please be careful of that! - It's the latest Mac Air laptop!

Karl   I can see that. Must've set you back a bit.

Tony   You get what you pay for: Macs are infinitely better designed than PCs.

Karl   Of course, design is everything. But aren't you worried about the dust? Don't you think it's a bit weird having all this ultra modern stuff in the middle of this mess? I mean this isn't a flat, it's a refugee camp. And the flies! Like being buzzed by Stukas! That's what you are Tony, a refugee in your own house! A refugee on the road to nowhere!

Tony   I'm not on the road to nowhere: I live here!

Karl: Not for much longer, if the agents see this place.

Tony   What agents?

Sophie   Karl!

Karl   Sophie told me she's got to do a report.

Sophie   No, I did not! Ignore him, Tony.

Tony   What report? I don't want anyone reporting on me.

Karl   Well then you'd better mend your ways.

Sophie   Oh for chrissake!

Tony   Are you from the council?

Karl   Do I look like I'm from the council?!

Tony   People aren't always what they seem.

Karl   Now there you're right, Tony! Wow: nice shredder! Canon?

Tony   Kodak, actually.

Karl   *(reading the box)* Ah yes! The 'SP 100 Super – multi-function - Suitable for small offices – What do you need this for?

Tony   Why does anyone have a shredder!? I've got documents.

Karl   Documents!? I can't see any documents. I mean I can see a lot of rubbish, but no... - no documents.

Tony   They reveal my identity.

Karl   *(Pointedly grammatical)* To whom?- I don't see anyone.

Tony   Identity theft is a very real problem: you should shred your documents too!

31

Karl   I should do a lot of things. But really - who'd want to read this rubbish?

Tony   It's not rubbish!

Karl   It is – manifestly – rubbish! It's the definition of rubbish. Look at it: piled high: a rejected, unsorted, unopened, unlooked at, unprocessed wasteland of rubbish! That's my point, Tony: you're not processing anything! This rubbish is a symbol of your whole life!

Sophie   Karl, I'm going out. Tony, I suggest you do the same until Karl gets off his psychoanalyst trip! *(but she doesn't move)*.

Tony   My life is not rubbish!

Karl   Well what is it then?

Sophie   *(To Karl)* Did you hear me?

Karl   *(To Tony)* You don't go out. You don't see anyone. You don't work.

Tony   I do work.

Sophie   Oh for Chrissake, That's it! I'm leaving! - Half an hour and I expect you *both* to be ready to help me again! I mean it.

Sophie goes to the door, but turns round to see if her departure has had any effect.

Karl   So what work is it? That you do do, I mean?

Tony   I'm a consultant for London Underground, if you must know. – Anyway, what business is it of yours who I work for, and when I work for them? Mind your own business!

Karl   I *am* minding my own business, Tony: here it is: and it's rotting. You're rotting. …And the crazy thing is you feel no shame.

Tony   How dare you ---

Karl   'An absence of shame' – or rather of 'the function' of shame - that's what they say about hoarders.

Tony   I am not a hoarder!

Karl   "A lack of any societal connection", Tony, of any awareness, any evaluation of what other people might think. So that in the end you end up with no friends.

Tony   I do have friends!

Karl   No work. Nothing. Your life is nothing – except a pile of rubbish.

Tony   Take that back!

Karl   You've got nothing! You keep nothing except rubbish. No, correction! You've got a shredder. – which you don't use. Maybe you don't know how to use it?

Tony   'Course I know how to use it!

Karl   Then let's do it together: how's that? We could shred the whole room! Every last statement and receipt! Come to think of it, let's shred the wallpaper too: and these old clothes: will it take them too? Let's give it a try! Shove it all in, lock stock and barrel. Put it out of its misery! Come on, we could be finished by Thursday!

Tony   I *do* use my shredder.

Karl   What for? There's no paper in it!

Tony   That's not true: I shredded a batch of British Telecom bills only yesterday.

Karl   One down – three million to go!

Tony   You don't understand: they take time to analyse!

Sophie takes a couple of steps back into the room.

Sophie   Karl! *(to Tony)* Tony, don't listen to him: you don't *have* to listen to him. - Karl, I know you think you're helping but it's cruel. You're just being cruel.

33

Karl No-one's asking you to stay.

Sophie glares at Karl then exits turning over a chair and slamming the door.

Tony There, now see what you've done.

Karl She'll be back. Meanwhile we can get on with shredding your room.

Tony I'm not listening to this! - I employ you!

Karl What?

Tony To clean my flat! I pay you to clean so I can get on with more important things!

Karl And just what might they be? *(desultorily picking through pieces the of hi-fi and TV apparatus)* Listening to the Beach Boys. Watching ten hours of telly a day?

Tony Please don't touch those! They're all set to record.

Karl Record what?

Tony Stuff.

Karl Stuff? What stuff?

Tony Stuff I like to watch.

Karl But you don't have to record stuff these days, Tony: you can watch it all on I-player; Channel4 On-Demand, you know: "you need never miss a show again'!

Tony Not the stuff I want to watch.

Karl What stuff would that be? Don't be coy, Tony. There's no need to be ashamed of a bit of porn these days. A middle-aged man on his own: you'd be odd if you didn't look at it now and then. So what's your preference? Young Asian models? Latino beauties?

Tony Look I know what you're trying to do!

Karl   Schoolgirls?

Tony   You're trying to make me admit to things. Well I won't.

Karl   Why not?

Tony   Because I don't have to. Not to you. Not to anyone. I don't have to because I haven't done anything wrong!

Karl   Who said you had?

Tony   You did!

Karl   Are you sure?

Tony   Yes, you did. You tried to say I watch stuff. Evil stuff. You're trying to make me out as some kind of pervert!

Karl   Well are you?

Tony   Fuck you! You don't know who I am or what I do – or –

Karl   But that's the point Tony, I'm trying to find out! I want to know what sort of person lives here! In this mess! In this disaster area you call a home! I mean you can't say it's normal.

Tony   Who wants to be normal?

Karl   I do Tony! When I stand here in the middle of this shithole I want to be as normal as possible. This place, the way you live makes me want to run to the normalest place on earth and never open my door again. - Because it frightens me, Tony. If you want to know the truth. I'm not happy standing here with you. Being in this room gives me the creeps. *You* give me the creeps. How can you live like this? *Why* do you live like this?

Tony   It's my home!

Karl   It's not a home! A home has rooms you can walk in, spaces to stretch out in! Lie down in! Make love in! Work in! Write in! Play music in! Dream in! - What can you do in here?! There's no room for anything!

Karl cont.   You've left no room! There's no room for a life! - You don't want to live? Is that it?

Tony   There *is* room!

Karl   For what?

Tony   Everything!

Karl   Such as?

Tony   Anything I like.

Karl   Yes but what *do* you like, Tony? You must do something with your time! How do you construct a day out of - this chaos? What is it you actually *do* with your life?

Tony   I…

Karl   Yes?

Tony   I…

Karl   Well? Tell me!

Tony   I….

Karl   For Chrissake, Tony!

Tony   Lots of small things!

Karl   Jesus…

Tony   I potter!

Karl   What?

Tony   I like to potter. - I spend the day pottering.

Karl   You potter.

Tony   Yes, I achieve a lot actually.

Karl What, so you're the Harry fucking Potter of your own private Hogwarts, are you? Pottering around in your little magic den. Well, I'll tell you one thing Tony, you need to wave a big fucking wand at this dump! No, actually, Tony, scrub that: - at your whole fucking life! Expeliamus, Tony! Big time!

Tony What are you talking about? You talk rubbish!

Karl Well you should like that, Tony: that should make you feel at home, shouldn't it? My talking rubbish? My words are furnishing you in your favourite style!

Tony I haven't got time for this! I've got things to do.

Karl No, you haven't. You've got all the time in the world! Just to wallow! Your job is to wallow in rubbish!

Tony Look, please stop ---

Karl Drown yourself in this sea of muck, this wasteland of anonymous bullshit just so you won't be able to find yourself. Maybe I was wrong about identity.

Tony Please – *(blocking his ears)*

Karl Maybe it's the opposite! You think if you hide your personality behind enough bits of paper you'll lose track of yourself completely – of who you've become! That's it, isn't it?

Tony No. No. No.

Karl - Because who you've become is repellent, isn't it Tony? So monstrous you can't even imagine how it happened to you! Can't believe it *has* happened to you! I mean, is *this* really you? Are these letters addressed to you? Is this your name? Maybe it's not! Maybe if you leave enough letters unopened it won't be your name anymore! You won't *be you* anymore. Your life won't *be* your life!

Tony No!

Karl And how convenient that would be!

Tony No… *(begins to sob)*

Karl How easy… - Just to let it all go! All the blame, the self-disgust! Let it all float away on the tide – get swallowed up in this sea of shit. Forget you exist, forget you have any responsibility to find out who you are! That's your identity crisis, isn't it, Tony? You're not worried about anybody else stealing it, you're worried about finding it!

Tony (sobbing) Please. *(Karl picks up a batch of letters next to Tony).*

Karl But life's not like that, is it? Life doesn't let us off the hook. - It pins our identity right there on our hearts! Woops, what's this? Another letter addressed to Anthony Morris of Golders Lane, Putney, E8 1BY – letter after letter after letter! *(He drops them onto Tony)*

Tony Throw them away! I don't want them!

Karl And the newspapers! *(gathers a handful and hurls them at Tony).*

Tony Stop!

Karl They're not protecting you: they're suffocating you! Look, you're drowning in wave after wave of meaningless words! A foetid sea of printed opinions!

Tony Please!

Tony Shall I throw them all away – the magazines too, the camera magazines?

Tony Yes!

Karl Really?

Tony Yes! Yes!

(Pause)

Karl No. *(Beat)* - Only if you throw them away with me, Tony! Otherwise it doesn't work.

Tony I can't!

Karl Yes you can! Stop hiding, Tony. Come out from behind them. You can throw them all away... stand here – and just... - be you...

A pause during which Sophie suddenly re-enters, speaking as she does so.

Sophie Yes, I know I'm back early, but then I thought why should I.... *(suddenly sensing the awful mood)* Karl, what's happening? What are you doing?

Karl Me? I'm not doing anything. It's Tony. He's going to throw everything away and start again, aren't you Tony?

Tony gets up and moves a few paces behind Karl and distractedly picks through objects on his desk. Standing behind Karl he examines the snow globe.

Karl Tony has finally realised he's got to make a change – haven't you, Tony?

Sophie Tony...?

Just as Karl turns to face him, Tony brings down the 'snow-globe' on Karl's head. He collapses. Sophie cries out ---

Karl!

Lights.

End of Act 1.

Optional interval

Act 2.

Same room. A few minutes later. Darkness. The sound of a shredding machine on automatic as it comes to the end of its run. Then silence. Lights up. Karl is seated in a chair, his legs tied to its legs; his wrists bound together in front of him, his head unconscious on his chest. Sophie is also seated very still in a chair as Tony is anxiously, slightly roughly, but not violently, tying her wrists to the arms of the chair.

Sophie   Tony, please – don't do this.

He tightens the knot, she winces.

Tony   Look, sit still, Sophie, I'm trying *not* to hurt you! I just need you out of the way for a minute while I deal with him. – Good to see he's shut up at last! *(pause).*

Sophie   Tony, I promise you I had no idea he was going to say those things!

Tony   Oh no, I'm sure you didn't exchange two words about me all the way here, did you? *(beat)* I trusted you, Sophie. And you bring this - Karl! - this churl into my home and suddenly I'm being interrogated!

He walks over the shredder, picks up a piece of paper.

The truth according to British Telecom! *(he feeds it in)*

Karl emits a soft moan.

Sophie   Tony…

Tony   Please … I'm trying to concentrate.

Sophie   He needs a doctor.

Tony goes over to inspect Karl's head.

Tony   It's OK, there's no blood - well, hardly any. I've put a small bandage on. He'll be fine. I didn't hit him hard. If it makes you feel better I'll call the surgery, they know where I live. *(He picks up a phone, dials and*

40

carries on speaking to Sophie) I just wanted to shut him up for once in his life! *(puts the phone down)* – Engaged. I'll try again in a minute. - I'll get him some water.

Karl begins to stir.

Sophie   Karl..?

Tony brings Karl a glass of water, sits him slowly upright and holds the cup so that Karl can sip from it, which he does.

Karl   My head… *(Suddenly realising the position he's in, comes round a bit more and struggles)*

Tony   Please sit still.

Karl   Fuck – what happened?

Tony   I think you'll find you're tied up for a moment.

Karl   Jesus..!

Tony   'Otherwise engaged,' you could say.

Karl   Get me out of this! Sophie --- !?

Tony   Oh that's typical: ask the woman to get you out of the mess you've made! Look, the sooner you sit still and listen to what I've got to say, the sooner we can all go home – well, I *am* home – but you know what I mean. That's the trouble with your type, Karl, you've always got to be in control. But you're not. Not in my home - and that's what I want to talk to you about.

Sophie   Tony, not now ---

Tony   Yes, 'now!' I decide – not you! It won't take a minute… *(beat)* It's really only a question of good, old-fashioned manners: how to behave in other people's homes – how to treat them, what to say – and what *not* to say, eh Karl? I mean, your generation is so hot on all that sort of thing: not offending people, using offensive words – you and your 'partner' here.

Tony cont.

'Partner!' I ask you! What sort of partner is he anyway, your Karl? Partner in crime? Business partner? I mean 'business partner' makes sense, it has legal status: - you know where you stand. But 'partner' - for a love affair? What's wrong with 'boyfriend'? or 'man' – or 'lover' even? –- If you ask me, partner's a word for people who can't commit themselves to a real status, you know what I mean? Marriage and all that.

Sophie is silent. Tony continues.

No, that's far too old-fashioned for Karl, here… - Karl the churl…

Karl   I think… I'm bleeding…

Sophie   Tony, please.

Tony   Stop ordering me around! I'm *trying* to get him a bloody doctor! They don't just come at the drop of a hat these days. You have to be practically dead before they bother with you! *(to Karl)* And you're going to feel a total lemon when the doctor does come and you tell him you've just got a headache.

Sophie   For chrissake, Tony – you hit him!

Tony   I know, I know. I'm sorry. *(beat)* I broke my snow-globe… didn't realise it'd be so fragile. *(he goes and pick up the pieces)* Got to mend it. I know it's cheap but it's got sentimental value. My mother got it from Helsinki ---

Karl   *(he can't help his sarcasm)* What, when she was a spy?

Sophie shoots a warning look at him.

Tony   What?

Sophie   He said 'why'.

Karl   Why what?

Sophie   Why was she in Helsinki?

Karl Oh I can't talk about that. Not here, not now – in his presence. He wouldn't listen anyway. Won't let you get a word in edgeways. *(to Sophie)* How do you bear him?! Firing all those bloody questions at you! Like a machine gun! Can't hear yourself think!

Karl I'm sorry.

Tony What?

Karl I'm sorry… - if I made you angry…

Sophie (carefully) Tony… just let us leave.

Tony In a minute! - Besides! You haven't finished tidying up! - And I haven't finished shredding! – I'll try the surgery again…*(He dials while still shredding very small pieces of paper).* Another British Telecom bill! *(reads it then begins shredding it)* Hold on: four hundred and sixty six quid? For a quarter?! What are all these premium numbers? I never called 'em! HMRC? – That's outrageous! Three calls to the taxman – a hundred and eighty of your English pounds! For what? To get a fifty quid rebate! How can that be right in a sane universe! And this! Speaking Clock £23.45 pence! – "The time sponsored by Tony Morris is… too bloody expensive" – that's what it is! – No - *(slams phone down)* they're still Engaged. Bet that's cost me twenty quid just hanging on for your unnecessary appointment, Karl! Actually, identity theft aside, you can tell a lot about a person from their telephone bill: the people they ring, when they ring them - can't tell *'why'* though: now *that would* be interesting! A biographical phone bill! - '9.28. p.m. July 11, Putney, 5 minutes 14 seconds, £2.13 pence – gave mistress quick call behind wife's back! ' - Even you'd shred that, Karl, wouldn't you!?

Karl I don't have a shredder.

Tony Ah no, I forgot: you're the man with nothing to hide! I tell you what! While we're waiting for the doctor, let's see you prove it, let's see *you* answer a few questions!

Sophie Tony…

Karl *(To Sophie)* I'm all right.

Tony There, you see? He's all right. Look, I'll take him to A and E after we've finished. Taxi service! Even wait with him! How about that?

Karl I don't need to go to A and E and I don't need a doctor.

Tony Oh now there I can't agree: you *should* at least get checked out, Sophie's right. If you lose consciousness – even for a second – you should always get it checked out. - I'll take you when we've finished.

Karl Finished what?

Tony Answering my questions. You asked me some: now it's my turn.

Karl I need a cigarette.

Tony I don't smoke, I'm afraid: fire risk with all this paper around. So! What to ask? Not so easy when you're put on the spot! I mean we don't even know each other really, do we? Not that that stopped you asking me questions! All right then! Something that means a lot to you. - Sophie! Your relationship with the woman you love – or say you love. – Do you love her?

Karl Of course.

Tony Of course. Well that's good. That's as it should be between people who've lived together for..? How many years? *(silence)* – Well?

Karl Ten. Eleven.

Sophie Thirteen.

Karl Off and On.

Tony Off and on. What does that mean?

Sophie It means sometimes we lived together and sometimes we didn't.

Tony - And sometimes you loved her and sometimes you didn't.

Karl   I always loved her.

Tony   And you always *will* love her? No, that's not a fair question. I retract that. No-one can say how they will feel in the future. The important point is you love her now. And you wouldn't be unfaithful to her. *(silence)* Well?

Karl   I would try not to be... *(Karl and Sophie exchange looks.)*

Tony   - Ah... so you *were* - once!

Karl   What's it got to do with you?

Sophie   Tony, please stop this ---

Tony   Yes, it's unpleasant isn't it? *(To Karl)* Well? What was her name, this lover of yours?

Karl   What does it matter what her name was?

Tony   Oh, I'm sorry, am I digging up bad memories? I wouldn't want to open old wounds. Sophie, I'm sorry if this is painful for you, but Karl insists on honesty!

Karl   Between friends!

Tony   And I'm not your friend?

Karl   Friends don't tend to bludgeon each other with blunt objects.

Tony   I was trying to help you.

Karl   If only I'd known.

Tony   - Teach you some bloody manners.

Sophie   *(deadpan)* Sarah.

They both turn to look at her.

That was her name. – the last one.

Karl Sophie –

Tony Ah, Sarah… One-night stand, was she?

Karl No-one uses that phrase any more.

Tony Oh sorry if I'm being old-fashioned.

Sophie And before that, Rebecca – but she wasn't serious.

Karl None of them were.

Tony I knew it! A womaniser is what you are! A serial bull-shitter!

Karl It didn't mean anything.

Sophie It lasted a year.

Tony Just sex, was it? - Come on, Karl, you can tell us.

Karl It's none of your business.

Tony I'm making it my business – the way you made my life your business! So what was it? Good old-fashioned lust? A one-night stand that went on a year? What?

Sophie Actually, Tony - we both had affairs.

Tony What?

Karl Sophie, don't.

Sophie Why not? What've we got to hide, Karl? If he wants to hear the intimate details.

Tony Steady on – I didn't mean *that*. I'm not a bloody voyeur.

Sophie We've been together a long time, Tony; things happen.

Tony Yes, but who's to blame for them? That's what I want to know.

Sophie Untie me and I'll tell you…. *(Tony hesitates)* You really expect me to discuss it like this?

Tony Fair enough… but *he* stays where he is. I haven't quite finished with him yet.

Tony starts to untie Sophie.

Certain things cannot go unsaid. Though, god knows, I'm a tolerant sort.

Karl Huh! What would you know about tolerance?

Tony What would I know? A lot, actually: *(he breaks off untying Sophie, who looks exasperatedly at Karl)* I tolerate you! I tolerate you coming into my house and tearing me apart in front of your 'partner'! – someone who, incidentally, I trusted; someone who brought you into my house! You with your bullshit affairs and your bullshit rock group and your bullshit guitaring! *(To Sophie)* So this is the man you want to live with for the rest of your life, is it Sophie? This 'three-chord wonder'! You want *him* to be the father of your children? A bloke who says he loves you while he fucks other women.

Karl I don't f … – sleep with other women.

Tony Yes you do. We just had a list!

Karl I mean, not all at the same time.

Tony Oh well that's very decent of you! Very orderly. Very sequential.

Karl You heard what Sophie said! These things happen. People grow apart.

Tony - And then conveniently fall back together again when it suits you.

Karl We've apologised to each other! It's nothing to do with you! – Look, can we just forget all this. I'm sorry if I upset you.

Tony   - 'if' you upset me? Oh yeah: the new form of apology: make it sound as if the offence is a matter of opinion: 'I'm sorry if you *think* I cut your head off with an executioner's axe…' Well, you certainly *did* upset me!

Karl   I said I'm sorry.

Tony   Yeah but you're not, are you? Not really. You're not *any* of the things you say you are. You're not clever. You're not kind. You just like hurting people. - Making me out as some kind of basket-case! Some pervert. I'm *not* mad. Sophie knows I'm not. - I know what mad people are like. I don't dribble. I don't sit in a corner mumbling. Spilling my food. I go out - I shop - I use a computer - debate. Art! Politics! You ask Sophie! She's been here a lot without you. Her and Suzie cleaned my flat brilliantly from top to toe. We get on, don't we, Soph'? Discuss painting! Abstractionism. Brush techniques. Jackson Pollock. Willem de Kooning! So don't paint me as some kind of lunatic. I won't be painted as a lunatic.

Sophie   We're not painting you as a lunatic, Tony.

Pause as Tony begins to calm down again.

Tony   Maybe I'm a bit .. eccentric. I accept that.

Karl   That was the word Sophie used… - about you: she never said you were mad.

Tony   So you *were* talking behind my back.

Sophie   Everyone talks behind everyone's back, Tony, it's called being human.

Karl   Sophie's always been kind about you.

Tony   *(cynical)* Oh yeah? *(Looks at Sophie)*

Karl   She said you were 'sweet', if you must know.

Tony   Really.

Karl   Said the hoarding was.. what was it? – 'a minor eccentricity.'

Tony   Yeah, well, as I say, I can be a bit eccentric… but that doesn't change what you said. Those other things: you can't just say take them back. What's said is said. Gossip never dies – it always comes back to haunt you. You said it: you think I'm a lunatic – worse, a pervert: you think I should be locked up just because I don't keep my room tidy.

Sophie   He doesn't.

Tony   Yes he does! He thinks the agency should chuck me out of my home!

Sophie   No.

Tony   Don't lie – or I won't untie him. *(beat)* Anyway, how would you know *what* he thinks of me? Tell me that! You don't even know what he thinks of *you* – this 'partner' of yours! How do you know he loves you? How do you know he hasn't got his eye on the next girl already?

Sophie   I know he loves me.

Tony   Funny way of showing it: fucking other women.

Karl   For god's sake ---

Tony   - Oh! for God's sake, is it? Well that really is devoted - religious, even! 'Karl, the man who fucks for God's sake!' – well I'll tell you what, Karl: God created the universe on his own: I think he can get his leg over without your help! - No, I'd suggest you fuck very much for yourself, Karl! Because that's what you are – a fucker who fucks people up and then fucks off!

Goes over to Karl.

Karl the churl! You're lucky I only hit you once! *(In his face)* You're lucky I'm *not* angry anymore. Jesus, I know people who who'd sit you here and beat you 'til you begged them to stop! – Oh don't worry - I wouldn't waste my energy..! Anyway… - torture doesn't work. – I saw it in a documentary on Pol Pot. Do you know why? *Karl shakes his head.*

49

Tony cont. - Because people will say anything under duress – just to stop the pain. So it follows that when they confess under torture, the information might be rubbish. So you might as well not torture them in the first place. 'Course that's not why people torture people, is it Sophie?

Sophie remains expressionless.

No, torturers aren't interested in getting the truth. They torture people because they just enjoy hurting them: they might say they're doing it for some cause or information, but actually they just enjoy inflicting pain. *(looking at Karl)* - Like you wanting to hurt me. *(looking at Sophie)* And he says he wants to help me!? I ask you! Help me by –*(turns to Karl)* - what was it?

Karl What was what?

Tony   That phrase you used? - Some clever bloody phrase - 'Exposure therapy' that was it! Looked it up, did you? Looked *me* up on Wikipedia? I bet you did. I bet you look everything up on Wiki-bloody-pedia! What can't be looked up on Wikipedia isn't worth knowing for people like you, is it, Karl! Well, I tell you what: *(he goes to computer and punches in something on keyboard)* - I'll look *you* up and I'll tell you what *I* think! - Karl ….. I'm sorry, I don't know your surname?!

Karl Jacobs.

Tony Jacobs… Good Jewish name. Noble race. Put up with a lot. You're letting them down, Karl - even as I Google you… - Karl Jacobs: rock star… rock star… rock - star! - Nope! I can't see you anywhere….. No entries at all in under 0.76 seconds! Not even in good old Wikipedia! Ah, unless you're Karl Jacobs, professor of bio-genetics at Stanford University, California? No, I didn't think so either. Hold on, wait! Yes! You *are* on Facebook! Karl Jacobs is on Facebook! Is that you?

Karl Yes. No. - I don't know.

Tony   What? You do know or you don't know if you're on Facebook?

Karl   Yes, I'm on Facebook. But it may not be me.

Tony What? 'You' might not be 'you'? Now where have I heard that before?

Karl People with the same name, I mean.

Tony Well I tell you what, Karl: let's not even bother to look, shall we? Because, truth is, I don't give a flying fuck whether you're on Facebook or not! I'm sorry to sound indifferent, but I'm just being honest, and honesty is always the best policy! Christ, I need a cup of tea! Does anyone else want a cup of tea? I'm desperate.

Sophie Let me make you one.

Tony Would you mind? That's be really kind. Karl, do you want some tea?

Karl (*deadpan*) Yes, a cup of tea'd be very nice, thank you.

There is a heavy pause as nobody moves.

Sophie So...

Tony What?

Sophie Are you going to untie me?

Tony Oh yes – sorry! Thought I had!

Finally he unties her and Sophie gets up, stretches and moves towards the kitchen area to get the tea things together. Tony eyes her movements carefully.

Tony Bit of peace and quiet for a minute. God knows, I've been wittering on a bit. Becoming self-obsessed. Maybe you've rubbed off on me, Karl! God knows what it must be like living with him? I'll bet you can't hear yourself speak! Well, tea all round, I say! All this excitement's worn me out. Here, I'll tell you what! This is classic situation comedy: you could write a play about it – about us, Sophie!

Sophie (*acerbically*) Maybe I will.

Tony   There, you see, Karl: our fifteen minutes of fame!

Sophie   After all, I've never been held prisoner before.

Tony   Oh no: that's not fair – you're not a prisoner: more a… witness.

Sophie   To a kidnap.

Tony   No!… - to an act of revenge – justice! I am *not* a kidnapper – It's not accurate. It's not an honest description of events. And that's what we need here: an eye for detail, the vital brush-stroke on the portrait. I should've thought you'd see that, with your painterly eye, Sophie. – Hey that's a point! Maybe you should paint us instead!

Karl   Paint us? What the fuck is she supposed to paint?

Tony   A historical document – a moment in time! A sort of 'When-did-you-last-see-your-father' thing! Or maybe something more abstract? Raw emotion. An Auerbach portrait: a splurge of colour! Karl's face is half way there already! *(He roars with laughter at his own joke)*

Sophie   *(curt)* Look, Tony, what is it you want? We've said sorry. Karl's apologised. You hit him! And *he's* apologised. Now he needs help.

Tony   I want to know *you*, Sophie! The real you! What makes Sophie get up in the morning! Why does she paint? Why does she write? Why does she live with Karl the churl! Why did she come here with him today?

Sophie   Then you'll let us leave?

Tony   Probably…

Karl   What sort of a deal is that?

Tony   I'm not offering a deal. I hold all the cards here, Karl: you're – indisposed.

Karl   So if you're not offering a deal, why should she comply with your request?

Tony Because I say so! *(beat)* Didn't your mother ever say that to you...? *(beat)* Stop asking questions! It's my turn!

Sophie *(calmly)* Art.

Tony What?

Sophie I get up to make art. Paint, write poetry.

Tony Ah yes! Find some meaning in the madness! Now we're talking! Actually, we've never really talked about your poetry, have we, Sophie? Another side of you we've clearly not discussed. Rhyme, do they, these poems? Modern poets don't normally rhyme, do they? Why is that, I wonder?

Karl It's not relevant any more.

Tony I wasn't asking you..! - though you may have a point. Modern life has lost so much of its music – and rhyme's a kind of verbal music, I suppose.

Sophie Sometimes I use rhyme - it depends.

Tony On what?

Sophie Whether my feelings do.

Tony That's a strange thing to say.

Sophie Good definition.

Tony What is?

Sophie 'Poetry is a strange thing to say.' – Love, a sense of beauty – the loss of it… Jealousy, hatred. Loneliness ---

Tony You won't earn any money with that!

Sophie I don't want to earn any money with it.

Tony Dead art, poetry. 'Specially poems about loneliness. - Old hat!

Sophie I don't know, Tony: there's an awful lot of lonely people.

Tony *(snaps)* I'm not lonely – if that's what you're implying.

Sophie I'm not implying anything.

Tony Yes, you are - and in an underhand sort of way too! I'm learning more and more about you, Sophie, I must say.

Sophie Then we're all learning about each other, aren't we?

Uneasy pause.

Tony If you ask me the world'd be a bloody sight better if a few people *stopped* sharing certain feelings ---

Sophie Is there any point to life without communication, Tony? – Secrets. Intimacies. Situations like this...

Tony So you write about your secrets, eh? - Hold on? Surely that makes them *not* secrets? Surely that makes you... what's the word? Ah yes - a blabbermouth!

Sophie A poem is an open secret: sharing it makes the truth more powerful.

Tony looks at Karl bemused.

Karl *(ironically)* Don't look at me!

Sophie Take this... You could say *this* place is an open secret. – Between the three of us. At least it could be – if we read it the right way.

Tony Yes well you can read too much into things! If you ask me you should choose a different subject to write about. – if you actually *want* any readers!

Sophie You don't choose the subjects you write about: they choose you.

Tony Then maybe you should blame them for your lack of success.

Sophie   I *am* successful.

Tony   Says who?

Sophie   I love writing.

Tony   What's love got to do with it? Hey, Tina Turner! Now there's a real goddess!

Sophie   If you love doing something, that's enough. You don't need anyone else's praise – or permission.

Tony   Bit selfish.. - Bit of a solipsistic universe you live in, Sophie.

Karl   *(under his breath almost as an aside)* Look who's talking.

Tony   What?

Sophie   *(Quickly interjecting)* - Not if what you write is beautiful – or true.

Tony   Ah but is it?

Sophie   Sometimes.

Karl   A lot, actually. *(from this point on, Karl is gradually, slowly freeing his hands from his ties)*

Tony   Oh well you would say that, wouldn't you – 'lover boy!'

Sophie   So what are you saying, Tony: that I'm wasting my time? I mean, you're always going on about not judging people; but doubt is a judgement.

Tony   I'm *not* doubting you!

Sophie   Yes you are.

Tony   I'm not!

Sophie   But when I tell you why I write, you don't believe me.

Tony   I do!

Sophie   You just told me you didn't!

Tony   When?

Sophie   In your tone of voice. Sneering.

Tony   I didn't!

Sophie   Oh yes you did!

Karl   *(tired, pantomimic)* Oh no he didn't…

Tony   I didn't! Look, if you say you write beautiful things I believe you!

Sophie   Why?

Tony   What do you mean ' why'? - Because you just told me!

Sophie   So if I told you 'to be or not to be' was a shitty speech you'd believe that?

Tony   Of course not. It's Shakespeare!

Sophie   A lot of intelligent people didn't like Shakespeare, Tony – Tolstoy! Voltaire! Dr bloody Johnson! You have to trust your own judgement… or you don't really exist.

Tony looks nonplussed.

Tony   Sorry?

Sophie   All that exists is someone else's version of you. You might as well walk around with someone else's name.

Pause. Tony turns to Karl.

Tony   Is she always like this?

Karl   Pretty much.

Tony   You confuse me, Sophie, you really do. I mean: you talk about honesty and lies; you do this job; you go home to a man who doesn't listen to you; write poetry that'll never be read. Jesus, no wonder you write about loneliness! You need an audience, girl.

Sophie   Maybe… maybe not. Maybe I've already got one.

Tony   Who?

Sophie   Not a person... - The silence.

Tony   Oh here we go!

Sophie   A blank page, a few words – The only thing that makes any sense.

Karl looks at her intently.

Karl   What about us? - Doesn't that make sense?

Sophie   I don't know: you tell me.

Pause.

Tony   You're right, Karl: *(looking at Sophie)* – she *is* a challenge! Well I hope art pays you back, Sophie, because you've made an awful lot of sacrifices. I mean, you could end up with nothing. You'd have Karl, but he's not exactly a guarantee of success, is he? Yes, you'd have your painting and your poetry, but no career, no nice home – no family! Don't you want a family? I mean, a woman of your age: you're leaving it awfully late, if you don't mind me saying so. Don't you want kids?

Sophie   Yes. - I do.

Tony   Well why haven't you had any? *(beat)*

Sophie   Because I want them - when *I* want them…

Tony   Well what if *they* don't want *you* when *you* want *them*? - What if they don't come at all?

57

Sophie   They will.

Tony   Really? How can you be so sure?

Sophie   I just know. - Like I knew before....

Tony   Mmm - sounds a bit... clinical - not to be rude or anything. – Have you had an abortion?

Karl   Oh Jesus!

Tony   What? It's just a question!

Karl   It's not '*just*' a question.

Tony   Yes, it is: you can answer yes or no: that makes it a question.

Sophie   Yes.

Tony   What? Yes, it's a question, or yes, you've had an abortion?

Sophie   Yes, I've had an abortion.

Tony   Ah. That explains a lot of things.

Karl   Listen, this really isn't --- !

Tony   Abortion's a difficult business.

Karl   I beg your pardon?!

Tony   Don't beg, Karl, it's embarrassing. *(to Sophie)* Was this recently, may I ask?

Karl   No you may *not* ask!

Tony   Well, put it this way: would you have another one?

Karl   Ignore him, Sophie!

Sophie   *(expressionless)* No.

Tony   There you are!

Sophie   I won't.

Tony   You see!

Sophie   I'm going to keep it.

A pause. Slowly the import of the tense she has chosen hits them both.

Karl   Sophie...?

Pause.

Sophie   *(deadpan)* You want me to, Karl, don't you?

Karl   Sophie…*(beat)*

Tony   She's pregnant!

Karl   Sophie what are you saying?

Tony   She's pregnant! – Sophie's pregnant!

Karl   *(Almost under his breath)* Oh my god.

Tony   Well this calls for celebration!

Karl   *(softly incredulous)* Sophie… Sophie..?

Sophie   *(cool)* What, Karl?

Tony   This changes everything!

Karl   How long have you known? Jesus! - How many weeks…?

Sophie   About eight, maybe ten, I'm not sure.

Karl   But you've done the tests - you're sure --- ?

Tony   Of course she's sure! Aren't you, Sophie?

Karl   For Chrissake shut up!

Tony turns on him.

Tony   Don't tell me to shut up! Don't *you* tell me anything! Don't you say a bloody fucking word! *(beat)* Sophie's sure: that's the main thing: she's going to have a baby… This is incredible. I don't know what to say. Well. Congratulations obviously! Let me get you some Champagne. I've got some somewhere. Just a glass won't harm you! Or the baby. Don't want to turn it into a boozer in the womb! I'll be back in a sec! *(As he goes)* - I'll get you a celebratory Paracetamol while I'm about it, Karl.

He exits.

Karl   Sophie, what the fuck's going on? *(At this point, his hands now free, Karl frantically unties his ankles)* - Help me out of this *(She helps him)* - When were you going to tell me for chrissake?!

Sophie   I don't know.

Karl   What do you mean: you don't know?

Sophie   I mean, I don't know. - Soon.

Karl   Soon?

Sophie   When it seemed right: I wanted to know how I felt, myself. - After last time.

Karl   So you choose *now* to tell me! Here: in this shithole, with this raving nutter?

Re-enter Tony. Karl automatically resumes a vaguely captive position, hands by his sides.

Tony   Here we are!

Sophie   I don't want any.

Tony   Oh come on: just a sip! It'll do you good. It'll certainly do me good! What about you Karl?

Karl   No.

Tony   Go on.

Karl   No, *(coldly)* - Thank you. ---

Tony   *(semi-menacing)* Have some.

Karl takes the glass Tony offers him. Tony doesn't seem to notice Karl's hands are obviously free.

Well! This really does change everything! Cheers! *(to Karl)* Look, I really am sorry. – I'll try the doctor again. *(He dials).* - And congratulations to you too, Karl! Ah hallo! *(gestures to them that he's got through to the surgery)* - Can you make an appointment for my friend to see the nurse, I've banged his head - correction! *he's* banged his head. Yes, this morning. No, he's not registered! He's visiting me and he needs to see someone. *(Pause)* No, just banged it on a cupboard… - it took the wind out of his sails. He had to sit down for a minute. He might have lost consciousness for a moment or two. No he doesn't want an ambulance. No, Look, forget that: He wasn't unconscious! No, not at any time! - He just needs to see the nurse. Well what time is the end of surgery? OK one o'clock'll be fine. *My* name? *(beat)* Morris, Tony Morris, 23 Goodbody Road, Putney. Yes. Yes. Yes. Thank you. *(hangs up)* Cow! I mean: *I know* if you lost consciousness or not! At no stage were you unconscious! Well, you *were*, actually, but that's not the point! *She* didn't know that! Yet there she was insisting you'd been out cold! Jesus! Put someone behind a desk and immediately they treat you like a fool. *(beat)* You treated me like a fool, Karl, and you weren't even behind a desk! Well I'm not: I'm completely normal. *(swigs champagne)* Cheers! - I know exactly what 'normal' is. I can do 'normal'. – I do everything a normal person does: except this *(gestures to rubbish)* - but I'm working on that. In every other way I'm normal. - Normal hopes, normal fears, normal disappointments – nelly bloody normal! I get on with it: - normally! Just like you, Karl! That's all I was trying to say back there! But you wouldn't let me… – Anyway! We're getting off the subject… -

Tony cont.   Cheers! Here's to Sophie and her new baby! Well! Wouldn't be an old baby, would it! Imagine that: if babies came out like fully-formed little old men! Mind you, some do, in a way, don't they? I mean you see some babies that really do look like little old men – and women! Old souls, they call them…. – Have you thought of any names? For the baby, I mean.

Sophie   No.

Tony   You've got to choose a name! Can't leave it without a name – even this early. What sort of names do you like?

Karl   We're not choosing a name here!

Tony   Why not? Here's as good as any place.

Karl   No, it's not.

Tony   What's wrong with it? - I mean, apart from the mess?

Karl   Everything! Look we'll choose a name when ---- What am I talking about? Why am I even discussing it? This is crazy.

Tony   At least try.

Karl   No!

Tony   All right, calm down. I'll start! What about Christopher? The saint of safe passage! No? Peter, then! Mmm, too conventional. You need something exotic. Xavier! That's a smart name for a boy. I've always liked that! What do you think? Come on. I'm making all the running. Something more traditional? Traditional, yet modern… - Jack! Perennial favourite! Comes top of The Times list every year! Jack – a captain of the team! Maybe too popular. All right, Tom! I do like 'Tom'. Simple. Strong, but kind. I'd like to have been called Tom. Never liked my name. Anthony! Mincing middle-class moniker! - Characterless! Suppose Tony's all right. Best of a bad choice. – Sylvester! Now there's an elegant name. 'Sly' for short. Though that is kind of ambiguous, I suppose! - Nice-sounding

Tony cont.   nickname, all the same: 'Oy Sly, how's it going?' – 'Nice one, Sly!' - 'Sly, you jammy bugger!" - Not that you'd say that to a child of course! Hmm. Maybe not Sylvester… - All right then…. What about….

At this point Karl suddenly rises and rushes at Tony, taking him down in a crash. Tony backs away on his haunches along the floor, momentarily terrified. Karl holds his wounded head. Sophie helps him upright.

Karl Let's get out of here! (*He rises. Tony starts picking himself up.*)

Tony Look what you've done! (*heaping up piles of cassettes and papers*).

Sophie   (*To Karl*) Can you walk?

Tony Go on then: leave! Both of you! Make your report! Tell them what you like! You're both liars anyway! (*To Karl*) – She didn't even tell you she was pregnant! That's how much she trusts you! And you, Sophie, Clinging onto this – this leech. Just *who* is holding *who* up? That's what I want to know! Yes, two babies having a baby, that's what you are. (*To Karl*) As for you! Rock star, my arse! *You're* the real hoarder here! Hanging on to your delusions!

Sophie   Tony…

Tony   Get out! Get out…!

Silence, during which Karl starts to look for his things, coat, wallet, etc.

Sophie   Tony ---

Tony   Leave me alone…

Sophie   No.

Karl   What are you doing?

Sophie   We're not leaving.

Karl   What? Have you gone mad?!

63

Sophie   And when we get home, what then?

Tony   Yes! - 'what then'?

Sophie   We'll talk, won't we, Karl?

Karl   Of course, we'll talk!

Sophie   - Plan everything. - Discuss what to do, when to do it. I'll carry on working until it gets too much; you'll earn when you can, we'll register with the hospital, meet the midwife, go to ante-natal classes together…

Tony   If you need any help ----

Sophie   And then one evening you'll turn round and say maybe you're not sure…

Karl   No…

Sophie   Suggest a little time apart –

Karl   Of course not ---

Sophie   - A bit of space - to get some perspective… - like the last time.

Karl   That's not true! Look, I refuse to discuss this now!

Sophie   *(deadpan)* Why?

Karl   I'm not telling you how I feel *here*! In this place!

Sophie   Why not? Tony's right: it's as good a place as any. - Actually it's better!

Karl   What are you talking about? Look, let's get out of here! This place is insane.

Sophie   *(Calm)* No it's not. *(deadpan)* It's the sanest place in the world. You said this room needed some honesty - well, you know what you've built here, Tony, with all this - crap? *(tosses a few magazines aside)* - A confessional.

64

Sophie cont.   *(To Karl)* I'm going to have this baby - and you're the father…
(beat) - You'll *always* be its father.

Pause.

Karl   I can't believe this.

Tony   Maybe you ought to try…

Karl   *(To Sophie)* And your writing? Have you thought about that? The
time to think? Have your own thoughts? How's that gonna fit in with a
baby crying night and day?

Sophie   It doesn't.

Karl   Exactly!

Sophie   So I'll stop! – For a while… Women writers have had children for
chrissake!

Tony   Tricky balancing act! - "The pram in the hall is the enemy of art!"
(Sophie scowls at him) - from that literary quotations mag… - Cyril Connolly,
as I recall.

Sophie   Children grow up, Karl. Go to school. I'm not giving up painting,
writing *(beat)* – But I can't *not* be a mother. - If I turned round one day –
and it was too late…

Pause.

Karl   Look, I never said I didn't want to be a father: I said I don't know if
I'm ready.

Sophie   You don't have to *know*… - you just have to do it…

Pause. Suddenly Tony picks up the slack with concerted over-positivity.

Tony   You'll be fine! Of course you will. Sophie'll be a brilliant mother!-
(To Karl) And you, - you'll make a …competent father..! - I'd've loved a
dad that played the guitar! Bit of music in the house! Never heard any in

ours. We had a piano in the dining-room. One of those dark brown upright jobs. Never got played. – Every time I looked at it I didn't know whether to be delighted or depressed! I wanted to learn. Didn't have the co-ordination – never had any co-ordination! -

Pause.

Well – what a day! Well, morning, actually. It's not even lunchtime. Shall I get us some sandwiches? *(Beat)*

Sophie   I'm going now, Tony. I'm sorry we didn't finish the room.

Tony   Don't go!

Sophie   I'll get someone else to come for you.

Tony   I don't want anyone else to come!

He stands in her way.

Sophie   What are you going to do, Tony? Hit me on the head too? You've already rung the doctor once, you can't have two friends running into cupboards on the same day…

He stands aside.

Tony   You'll come back! In a couple of weeks - when you've had a rest!

Sophie   I don't think so, Tony. You need someone else. *(She gathers her cleaning equipment, etc)*

Tony   Let me help you with that.

Karl   I'll do it!

Sophie   Someone who doesn't interfere with your life.

Tony   I *want* to be interfered with! Well, in a manner of speaking! Look, I'm going to change!

Sophie   No, you're not Tony.

66

Tony   I am! - I'm going to tidy up this flat right now and begin again. No! first, you know what I'm going to do? To prove I mean business: I'm going to report myself to the police.

Sophie   Tony --- *(he takes up pen and paper)*

Tony   No! I insist! You said this room is a confessional, well I'm going to write a confession. It's the least I can do after belting Karl on the head with that snow-globe. Look, I'll read it out as I write it. – "I Tony Morris of –" I'll fill that in later – "confess that this morning, July 4th – ha! Independence day! - without provocation, hit Karl Jacobs with a snow-globe, and tied Sophie Woods up, and that I wish to receive help for anger management problems – amongst other things…" There! Where's the phone? *(hunts for it and talks to Sophie as he does so).* You'll still come..? - Clean for me, I mean? Later, I mean. There'll be a break, of course, while the baby's a baby – but after that, you'll come back. - A few months down the line maybe, you could bring it – him – her whatever it is: here! I mean I'm not very good with toddlers, well who is? But maybe --

Sophie   Tony, Tony…. - Where could a child play here?

Tony   Well not here, obviously, but on the Green, it's only a few minutes.

Sophie   I've got a Green near me, Tony. Why would I need to come to your Green?

Tony   Because we're friends…

Sophie   Tony, I'm your cleaner! - I'm paid to come here. I clear all this away - and then *I* go away, and you make it all come back again – like a tide coming in…. *(beat)* I don't know why you live like this. Maybe you just let it drift one day too many; and all this *(sifts some papers)* time just heaped up. - But you're in here somewhere, Tony - you've just gotta find out which bit of paper matters and which doesn't… Same as the rest of us.

She looks at Karl. Sophie cont.   I'm going now. Come if you want – *only* if you want. *(Beat, then understated)* I love you. - We could be a family…*(She turns away and leaves. Long pause. Tony looks at Karl as the door closes.)*

Tony   We *are* friends. She *said* we were friends. We get on well – when she comes round and cleans, I mean… *(Pause)* - Well?

Karl   Well what?

Tony   Aren't you going to get her back!

Karl readies himself to leave, looking sardonically back at Tony.

Karl   Thanks for the advice. Look*(beat)* I'm sorry for what happened today.

Pause.

Tony   No. - I'm sorry I hit you. – I meant what I said about confessing to the police - Wait!

Tony picks up the phone, punches a number into it, then picks up his earlier confession.

Hallo, Putney police station? Yes, I wish to report an assault…

Karl approaches Tony as he continues on the phone.

 "Who by?" - By me. That's who! - My name is….

Karl   Tony…

Karl takes gently Tony by the arm, replaces the phone on the receiver, then takes the 'confession' from Tony's other hand, and staring Tony in the eye feeds it in the shredder. We hear the sound of the shredder start and stop as it completes its function. Karl picks up his coat, takes a swig of Champagne from a glass, winces, gingerly touches the back of his head and goes to the door. He turns briefly to look back at without expression. He leaves. Tony, stunned, stares at his departing figure as lights fade to black.

End.

Disposophobia

James Murphy

Front & back cover photo courtesy of Heretics Press
Front and back cover design
by Chris Derrick @www.unauthorizedmedia.com

www.ingramcontent.com/pod-product-compliance
Lightning Source LLC
Chambersburg PA
CBHW031526040426
42445CB00009B/412